Southern Lotu

LITTLE FUZZY
CUTE & EASY COLORING BOOK

COLORING

LET YOUR IMAGINATION RUN WILD!

Coloring takes us to a world where freedom, creativity, and self-expression really pop, giving us a fun break from all the modern-day stress. It has not just become a relaxing activity but a must-have in our daily routine.

----- SHARE WITH US! ---------

Your unique style makes every coloring page special. We'd love to see your creations! Drop some pictures with your feedback so we can enjoy the awesome work of a creative artist like you!

scan to join with us!

CONNECT WITH US

Please feel free to reach out to us if you have any questions.
coloring@southernlotus.com

1000+

FREE DIGITAL COLORING PAGES!
Grateful for your choice!

Scan the QR code
for free digital pages

Southern Lotus

Share your masterpieces with us.
Always look forward to your amazing creativity

@southernlotus.publishing

Southern Lotus Coloring Book

@southernlotus_publishing

@southernlotus.publishing

@southernlotus.publishing

@southernlotuscoloring

CONNECT, SHARE and LEARN

17:58

southernlotus.publishing

- Daily tutorials
- Coloring tips
- Free Artwork

Southern Lotus

southernlotus.publishing

Follow | Message

FOLLOW us on Instargram

scan us for more fun!

Southern Lotus

Relaxing video!

Coloring tutorial!

A LITTLE NOTE BEFORE COLORING!

We select standard-quality paper to keep our products affordable due to the limited options available on Amazon. If you experience bleeding with certain pens or markers, placing a blank sheet of thicker paper behind the page can help. We are grateful for your understanding.

blank paper

THIS BOOK BELONGS TO

....

Take an adventure to a fluffy and cozy land where little fuzzy buddies with soft fur and chubby cheeks gather for endless fun. Each day comes with giggles and funny discoveries as they enjoy their daily activities filled with love and friendship. Let's go!

TEST COLOR PAGE

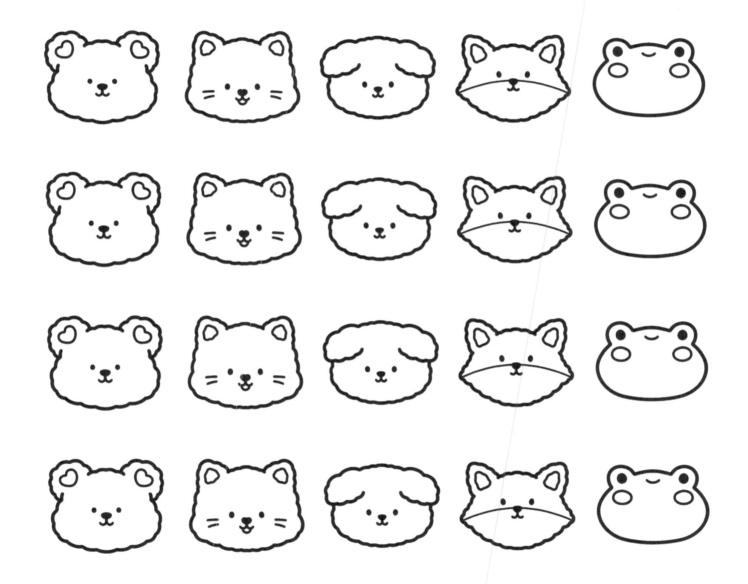

TEST COLOR PAGE

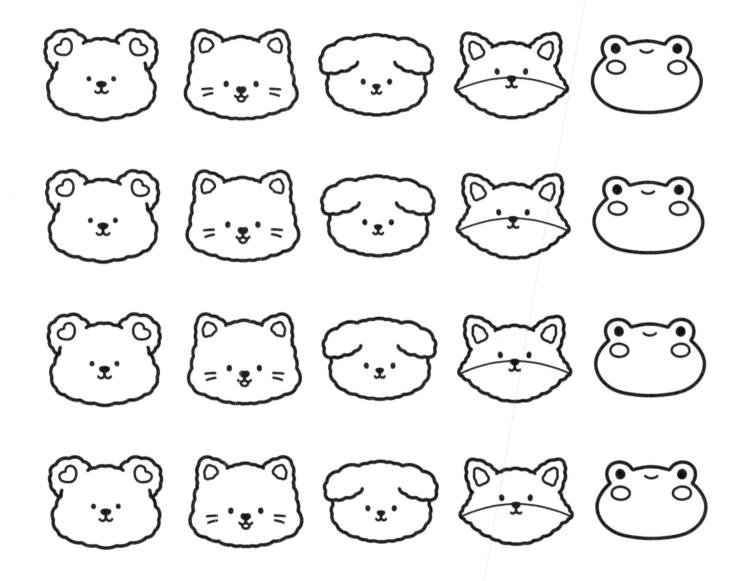

✂ -

Use this paper underneath to prevent ink seepage and maintain the integrity of your creation (Optional)

BOLD AND EASY COLLECTION

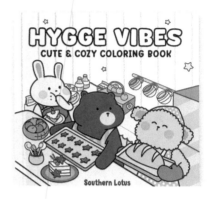

Made in United States
Troutdale, OR
11/16/2024

24887255R00058